I SHUDDER TO THINK, THEREFORE I AM

POEMS

by

PETER GALE

Dear Sarah,

It has been an absolute joy and a privelege to work with you. I hope we do so again one day, but next time, with some money attached and no rat poo!

With love and adneveration, Peter

X

(Gale)

YES OH YES PRESS

First published in 2004
by Yes Oh Yes Press, 4 The Close, Radlett, Herts WD7 8HA

Copyright © 2004 by Peter Gale

British Library Cataloguing-In-Publication Programme
A catalogue record for this book is available from the British Library

ISBN 0 9536126 0 0

Printed in Great Britain by
Woolnough Bookbinding, Northants

In memory of my dear nephew,
Luke Gale
1978–1999

To pull yourself together
When life tears you apart,
Buckle up with laughter,
Brace with wit your heart.

Contents

About Peter Gale

Born in 1941, Peter made his first London stage appearance in *Peter Pan* at the age of twelve, later winning the Gold Medal and the Ibsen Prize at the Central School of Speech and Drama. He is one of those rare, multi-talented performers, who is equally at home in musical theatre, the classics and new writing. His career spans the West End productions of *Cowardy Custard* (directed by Wendy Toye), *The Winslow Boy* (directed by Frith Banbury), *Hamlet* (directed by Tony Richardson), the London première of the Gershwins' Pulitzer Prize-winning musical *Of Thee I Sing*, the more recent UK première of Athol Fugard's *The Captain's Tiger* at Richmond Orange Tree and a new version of Camus' *Caligula* at the Donmar Warehouse (directed by Michael Grandage).

He has worked extensively in TV and film, notably in *The Darling Buds of May*, *Sense and Sensibility*, *The Merchant of Venice* and Steven Spielberg's epic film *The Empire of the Sun*.

He has written several programmes for BBC radio (three for Elaine Stritch), a one-man play, *Hopkins!* about the poet Gerald Manley Hopkins (British and American tours), a play, *The Unspeakable Crime of Maud Allan*, which he directed in Moscow, and a musical entertainment, *Side by Side by Shakespeare* which he has performed in Britain and Holland with Marilyn Hill Smith.

Introduction

When I was but seventeen, I became inspired to write inscrutable poems which were not bad. In fact, they were completely dreadful. But you only learn by doing, so I became an actor. However, it was the start of a lifelong passionate love affair with the English language. Years later, during the 70s, I organised a series of Christmas entertainments called *Bah! Humbug!* These were given in various London churches, mainly St-Martin's-in-the-Fields and St James's, Piccadilly, to raise money for various charities, and featured carols and readings performed by myself and friends, with star guests such as Julia McKenzie, Judi Dench, Derek Jacobi and Paul Hardwick (my partner for twenty years). Continually digging in the local library for new material for the programme was always great fun but I soon discovered that no comic poem I'd come across quite summed up my particular feelings about the dark gurgling underbelly of Christmas. A couple of amusing lines had been circling in my brain waiting for landing permission, so one afternoon I scribbled them down, just to see what would happen. Others followed, till a couple of days later the whole operation shuddered to a satisfactory halt and I realised I had written my first comic poem which I called *Stick Up Your Stockings! This Santa Is Loaded!* But lack of confidence in my personal muse – I was born in Slough, for goodness' sake – obliged me to attribute the poem to

Anon, flanked as it was in the programme by authors like Ogden Nash and John Donne. How *dare* I?

The day of the performance came. None of the cast queried the new poem but I was nervous. As Janet Suzman read it, my face went hot and red, and I became breathless and I trembled like a twig in winter. But Janet read the poem wonderfully, building the laughs to a final big one and receiving enthusiastic applause as she sat down. And that, I thought, was that.

However, the seal was broken and in subsequent recitals, when other actors read the poem, including Paul Eddington, Penelope Keith, Alec McCowen and Diana Rigg, I allowed myself the author's credit in the programme. Alec even asked me if I would allow him to perform it at other events. My bardic confidence thus plumped up, I wrote *Greek Ruins* for a one-man show I performed at the New End Theatre in Hampstead. Thereafter, ideas for poems presented themselves with variable results. A friend of mine, the actress Gay Hamilton, used a few short ones in a revue she devised with Kara Wilson. Her performance of *Sonnet 2001* was particularly enjoyed by the audience, some of whom, after the show, asked if they could buy my poems. And not just deeply concerned friends. Complete strangers. This volume is my response to their request and was made possible by the enthusiasm, help, advice and skills of the publisher Jeannie Cohen, to whom I was introduced by the artist Ros Bieber (who *is* a deeply concerned friend). My sincere thanks to you all.

Peter Gale, 2004

I SHUDDER TO THINK, THEREFORE I AM

Life, however sweet, soon discloses
That sometimes you get hurt, sometimes sick.
Even if it's one long bed of roses,
You have to put up with the occasional prick.

PERSONAL GROWTH

Your haunted glance of consternation –
Is it a sorrow bravely faced?
A secret, noble resignation?
No. A bunion tightly laced.

DON'T TELL ANYONE

Gossip doesn't bother me;
I'm eager to receive it.
What really shocks me rigid is
My readiness to believe it.

DON'T HOLD YOUR BREATH

"The world is going to know my name!"
She cried to strangers when she met 'em.
But when it came to finding fame,
She only went from strength to Streatham.

LOOK HERE

Where are my specs?
Oh where oh where?
> In bush, in briar?
> On chest, on chair?

By phone, by fire?
On top of TV?
> In tumble dryer?
> Oh come to me.

By towel in loo?
On roof of car?
> Oh call to me
> Where e'er you are!

Under a paper,
Above my face —
> They could, and will be,
> Any place.

I had them here
And now they've gone.
> Oh when did I
> Last have them on?

I put them down —
Now here's a clue —
> Beside my keys.
> And they've gone too.

They're hiding somewhere,
Mister Magoo,
      But where oh where?
      I wish I knew.

Don't panic. Think.
Just work it out.
      It doesn't help
      To yelp and shout.

In fact, you make
The problem worse
      The more you wail
      And growl and curse.

Let us for
A moment ponder —
      On whose legs
      Do glasses wander?

Freud would ask,
"Exactly who
      Invents this game
      Of peekaboo?"

Specs don't travel.
It's not voodoo.
      They don't do
      The hiding. *You* do.

Search yet again,
And then thrice more,
      By sink, by clock,
      By hat, by door,

By shoes, by soap,
By pad, by pen,
      I check and then
      I check again!

By shopping bag,
By TV book,
    By hook, by crook,
    I look and look.

On desk, on shelf,
In cupboard, in case.
    I think they've flown
    To outer space.

By hi-fi set,
By paper-bin.
    Behind things, on things,
    Under, in.

By diary, clock,
In bedroom, hall,
    In kitchen, loft,
    I've scoured them all.

In shorts, in shirts,
In coat, in mack,
    But specs they simply,
    Limply lack.

I am the world's
Completest looker.
    I even look
    Inside my cooker.

Down sofa cleavage
There was but
    Two coins, a nail-file
    And a nut.

With crazy stare
I've peered and gazed
    Until I'm gibbering,
    Stumped and dazed.

I'll make some tea
And have a rest.
         I open the fridge —
         I should've guessed.

In hunting specs
The hours I spend
         Would mount to years
         Placed end to end.

Immortal works
I might have penned,
         Instead of hunting
         Specs, my friend.

I am a-weary
Of the chase.
         I'll glue the damn things
         To my face.

Learn from me.
Avoid such frenzies.
         Go and purchase
         Contact lenses.

OBIT IN ORBIT

For stardom the human race was groomed.
It worked hard, learnt fast.
But alas, the great career was doomed.
It refused to speak to the rest of the cast.

THE WISE CRACK

Wood chips,
Bread crusts,
Silk slips
And marble busts.

> Paper flags,
> Plaster casts,
> Plastic bags;
> Nothing lasts.

The zip flies,
The organ stops,
The hair dyes
And the nose drops.

> The candle ends,
> The hairline cracks,
> And that my friends
> Is the life of facts.

PERFECT HELL

She was exercised by hell;
She didn't wish to go there,
Afraid to meet, as well,
The people she might know there,
The company she'd find.
It preyed upon her mind.
The noise, the smell, the heating.
And what about the seating?
The flames that lick,
The imps that prick,
The whole thing terrified her sick –
The length of time you spent there,
The awful sort who went there.
With every waking breath
It worried her to death.
She shuddered and said, "Oh,
I've no desire to go."

The torment was severe;
It plagued her night and day.
She lived in constant fear
Until she passed away.
She died quite peacefully in bed,
Then woke up with a start,
Filled with an awful dread.
"What's happened to my heart?
There's nothing there," she said.
"It isn't beating. Am I dead?

And if the answer's yes,
What is my address?"

Next thing the bulging clouds
Revealed angelic crowds
Singing to the Lord
With many a crashing chord.
All this, of course, she knew
Was quite a hefty clue.
Her face went very hot and red
For being self-indulgent.
The light about her head
Was unmistakably refulgent.

And so began eternal bliss
But sadly she grew used to this
And as she flew in the blue above
Her mind would stray below,
Wondering how the God of Love,
With sweet supernal features,
Could make a jail of pain and woe
For his created creatures.
Eternal hell did seem
A little too extreme;
A very odd beatitude
To take for mere ingratitude.
Maybe that place was not *all* bad,
Not *all* the time for *every*one.
Were there *no* pleasures to be had?
Not even perverted kinds of fun?
Maybe the flames and burning coals
So luridly illustrated,
Eternally punishing groaning souls,
Were slightly overstated?
She secretly longed to see
Exactly what went on there,

Till one day she, yes even *she*,
Wished that she had gone there.
She wished it then, she always will;
A million years, she'll be wishing it still.
For though she knows that she is blessed,
And here's the too familiar twist,
She frets without rest, completely obsessed
With what she might have missed.
She thinks of hell. She always will;
A million years, she'll think of it still.

And there our story concludes.
Her choir's conducted by Brahms.
She watches his waving arms,
And as she sings, she broods.
She broods on hell. She always will;
A million years, she'll be brooding still.
So that's what happened when she died.
Some folk are never satisfied.

WHAT IS THIS THING CALLED, LOVE?

The stiffness of the male erection
Often comes without affection.
Passion is a fierce addiction.
Sex itself is merely friction.

Hugs and squeezes
Spread diseases,
Swapping germs
On juicy terms.

Crazy, gross infatuation
Can become a mad fixation
Which in turn can lead to stalking
Persons innocently out walking,
Which is creepy and stealthy
And obviously unhealthy.

Lust
Is the opposite of disgust.
It's a blundering force that, on the whole,
Many men can barely control.
Though international,
It's irrational
And hence
Makes little sense.

Of the above, love is a layered blend,
But scratch the surface and you'll find a friend.

TAKE THAT, YOU ROTTEN SWINE!

You lazy cow,
You dirty dog,
Greedy pig,
Slimy frog,

You snake in the grass,
You selfish cat,
Stubborn mule,
Barmy bat,

You cold fish,
You timid mouse,
Crazy coot,
Stinking louse,

You silly goose,
You grumpy bear,
Pompous ass,
Stupid mare,

You slippery eel,
You sly fox,
Ugly trout,
Dumb ox,

You vicious animals,
Cruel brutes,
Forgive our meaner
Attributes.

With weasel words
And sheepish grins,
We ascribe to you
Our faults and sins.

We bitch and badger
And hound but find
The unkindest beast
Is the human kind.

THE ENEMY WITHIN

The HIV negative report
Gave them the positive go-ahead
To book the paradise resort
And nightly, nakedly share a bed.

A marriage on, and none too quick,
Came the catastrophic news.
The shocking error made her sick.
How could she have missed the clues?
The answer stared her in the face.
His squalid, homophobic views
That put her sharply in her place,
His tidiness to an eighth of an inch,
His lack of humour, insight, grace,
His bursts of rage that made her flinch,
His criticism of her breasts,
Her nose, her thighs and her behind,
His cruel jibes in front of guests,
His deadly, shallow, narrow mind
Hadn't shown up in the tests.

MARTIAL BLISS

Their marriage began in bed
But led to hell, not heaven,
Their favourite position not sixty-nine
But a very spread eleven.

FACIAL ATTRACTION

They wore their specs
While having sex,
Two naked souls
Blind as moles,
At it like knives,
Risking their lives,
Lenses clacking,
Sometimes cracking,
Achieving coition
With facial addition.

As they viewed
Each other nude
Through scholastic
Peeper plastic,
Clarified vision
Aided precision,
Placing grimaces
On furnished faces.

Contact lenses
In such frenzies
Wild and frisky,
Though less risky,
Just did not
Hit the spot,
But naughty games
In reading frames

In the buff,
Strangely enough,
Did the stuff.

Looking strict,
This couple clicked,
To coin a phrase,
In several ways,
The clattering
Hardly mattering.

They didn't mind
That love is blind.
They just preferred
It wasn't blurred.

DONG GIOVANNI

She loved music
By the spoonful,
Very sweet
And very tuneful.
She loved operas
Well sung
By fine tenors
Well hung.

WOMEN ARE FROM VENUS
MARSUPIALS ARE FROM MARS

I want a UFO.
I want one now, today,
To take me in its whirling disk
And whisk me far away.

A saucer I can sit inside
Steered by weird wee aliens,
Not mundane Danes in aeroplanes,
Or Strine strangling Australians.

A spaceship strangely silent
And glowing very bright,
Made of metal very smooth
And very strong but light.

One UFO to lift me
Inter outer space,
Although I've heard, when I get back,
I won't know what took place.

The people they abduct
Deny it's all a spoof
But give no detailed, clear account,
No evidence or proof,

No scientific facts
We don't already know
About the nature of such craft
And how they're made to go.

Those abductees are odd
To whom no thing attaches,
No drop of alien mud or blood.
I'd pinch a book of matches.

They come back with no mugs,
No tee shirts and no caps.
No wonder one is sceptical.
I want to see the snaps.

From infinitely far
Away those aliens fly.
They take one look, then off they go.
I often wonder why.

They must be very clever
The way they ride the sky,
And obviously curious
But singularly shy.

A wave or two would help,
A fraction more rapport would.
Though technically advanced, they're most
Backward in coming forward.

Perhaps they feel afraid
Of causing interference,
Or maybe sheer embarrassment
About their odd appearance,

But aliens don't chat.
How can they? They won't wait.
They know far more than we do, but
They can't communicate.

So where's my UFO
To beam me up today?
Although I won't remember much
I want one anyway,

A genuine UFO,
Dump me though it might
Empty-handed, disbelieved.
Where can I book a flight?

DENG XIAO-PING (1904–1997)

The supreme ruler of all China is dead.
His body was driven in a small minibus
To a graveyard for a brief, private burial.

A man who denied millions political freedom,
Even in death was afraid.

MY HUSBAND TED

My husband, Ted, when he gives way to lust,
He's just an animal. But only just.

WHODUNNIT?

The Agatha Christie doctor shook his head.
"Your husband, I regret to say, is dead."
He gravely placed his hands behind his back.
"The cause of death – a hatal fart attack."

THROUGH A BEER-GLASS DARKLY

"I have to pause.
I have to think.
I think I'll have
To have a drink

And after work
Another one
And then go on
As I've begun.

I think I'll say,
'It's getting late.
I'll have one more,'
And make it eight.

I think I'll fall down
In the gutter,
Sing a song
And sob and mutter.

I think I'll wake
The market place
And try to punch
A stranger's face.

I think I'll say
I really love him,
Then I'll violently
Shove him.

I think at home
I'll drink some more
And then I'll pass out
On the floor.

I think I'll wake up
With a head
And wish profoundly
I were dead.

I think tonight
That's what I'll do.
I think I'll have
A drink or two.

Tonight I think
I'll drink and drink.
That's what I think,
I think, I think."

And having thought,
He donned his hat,
And went and did
Exactly that.

THE PROPER STUDY OF MANKIND IS HOW TO FORM A QUEUE

Once upon a time, my little ones,
Long and *long* ago in olden days,
When there were phonographs and ha'penny buns,
Farthingales, lorgnettes and whalebone stays,
The glory of the Anglo-Saxon race,
A fine tradition, British through and through,
A national treasure given pride of place,
Was something termed – from Latin's 'tail' – The Queue.

The Queue was formed by people in a row,
Most notably while waiting for a bus.
One by one the queue would grow and grow
As each arrived – no cheating and no fuss.
And lo! – the first in line was first to mount.
The next was next, and this was named fair do's,
For those were called politely to account
Who jumped their place by ignorance or ruse.

And so it came to pass fairness prevailed,
Peace on earth, goodwill throughout the land.
Dignity and grace walked unassailed,
For there were Queues, as Heaven for Man had planned.
But that, alas, was long and *long* ago,
When folks did up their boots with button hooks,
And Christmas morning sparkled white with snow,
And everyone had butlers, maids and cooks.

Oh days of innocence, I mourn your loss,
For though our modern times have brought their pluses,
Such as flavoured crisps and dental floss,
None compares to queues once formed for buses.
That bygone custom is extinct today
And long forgotten too its arcane rules.
Folk simply gather now in disarray,
Much like a crowd of jostling molecules,

Not in a line but as a shapeless group,
Like clouds of water droplets formed by chance,
Or restless atoms in a heated soup,
Moved by convection in an aimless dance.
Some lurk in doorways, innocently near,
And, as the watched-for bus looms in the street,
Like fish at feeding time, quickly appear,
Darting to the front to seize a seat.

Oh then how dangerously thin the crust
On civilized behaviour's pinstripe suit!
How barely tamed and hungrily robust
Beneath the pretty, scented blouse the brute!
Specially when the tubes have gone on strike.
With mobile phones and bulging Filofaxes,
Travellers wage, bereft of car or bike,
The Battle of the Buses and the Taxis.

Our feet are washed, our toe-nails clean and clipped,
Shod in shiny shoes, not caked with dung
Like lowing herds in lorries being shipped,
Trampling on the old and weak and young.
But so the human animal is tested,
Driven by the challenge to survive,
To keep its individual hide invested
In the bid to stay alive and thrive.

Bacteria or beast, we all compete;
In jungle, ocean, office-block, we fight,
Doomed in war or peace, in stream or street.
Only the Queue can save us from our plight.
I mourn the bus queue's passing, little ones,
That emblem of a much more gracious age,
Before the need to curb the sale of guns,
Before the lethal link of road with rage.

Those days of rotten teeth but lofty speeches,
Open sewers but no gutter press,
Stinking drains but unpolluted beaches,
Lunatic asylums but no stress,
When yeomen yeoed with loyal oaken hearts,
And viscounts' robes were ermine, not fake fur,
And if you robbed and killed in foreign parts,
Queen Bess would take her cut and dub you Sir.

Those were the *good* old days. Who says they weren't?
When knights wore tights and maids weren't made till
                                    wedded,
When lords wore swords and holy saints were burnt,
And trouble-makers publicly beheaded.
Today the Bus Queue is a rare antique.
The last I saw consisted of six nuns.
In crowded streets now blessed aren't the meek,
For they shall inherit the pavement, little ones.

TAKE YOUR MEDICINE LIKE A WOMAN

Though men are stronger,
Women live longer,
And generally don't complain as much,
Or moan about pain as much.
They consult their GP's more readily
While men sit at home grumbling insteadily,
Hence men's relative brevity,
And women's longevity.
Also, being testosteroneous,
Men are more felonious.

THE BELLE TELEPHONE

I ring Alisa. No, she isn't there.
Actual, positive sightings are quite rare.
Obediently, I listen for the beep
And leave a message, nothing that won't keep.
Nothing urgent. Simply touching base.
An echo logged and left in cyberspace.

> I love Alisa, my fairest friend of all.
> But this is the sound of Alisa returning my call . . .

THEY LUST THEIR WAY

For obvious reasons, men
Are most attached to their dicks.
That's why they stray from the narrow way
And act like perfect pricks.

A man is his own master?
It's not the case, dear reader.
When his id prevails and he jumps the rails
He's following his leader.

His head may be ship's captain
But his cock is the running tide,
And when it flows, away he goes
And will not be denied.

Both tide and roaring gale,
It overrides his steering,
As will and mind go deaf and blind
And looking turns to leering.

A limpid lake is reason,
A roaring rapid is lust,
And a man is daft to entrust his craft
To its wreckless, rampant thrust.

Deserting wheel and chart
He leaves them to his chopper,
Whose tiny brain is quite insane
And thus he comes a cropper.

He calls it his John Thomas,
His Hampton or his Willy.
By any name it smells the same
And drives its owner silly.

In France its name is Zizi,
In America it's Peder,
But anywhere, if nookie's there,
He's following his leader.

For the call is wild and clear
And echoes to his roots,
A magnetic pull to the grazing bull
Which drags him by his boots.

And so men lie their way
Through mazes of deception.
It's a shocking fact the way men act
And I am no exception.

Of caution, care and prudence,
Men have no contraception.
I swear to you, I know it's true,
For I am no exception.

      It's a waste of shame and time and blame.
      Thank God I'm no excepton.

IN PRAISE OF YO-YOS

My heart leaps up when I behold
Ye olde yo-yos being sold.
In this mechanical, cynical age,
Computer games are all the rage,
Inter-active, high-tech, smart,
Solid state and state-of-the-art.
Children, twitchy and obsessive,
Tense and murderously aggressive,
Hunch before surreal scenes,
Blasting opponents on glowing screens.
It's kill or be killed in pixel suspension
Alone in an antisocial dimension.

I'll tell you also what the matter is —
Batteries.
Those electronics don't come cheap
That twitter and bubble and squeak and bleep.
Yo-yos are classical, oldfangled fun;
Also the juice on which they run
Is an energy-conserving thing
Called string,
Though charmingly unscientific,
Ergonomically terrific.

Champion yo-yo demonstrators
Dazzle and delight spectators,
With flourishes and flicks and flings
And curling loops and scoops and swings;

And not a silicon chip in sight.
A mis-spent youth well-spent all right.
Applaud their whizzardry and ease.
Let's hear it for the yo-yo, please.

The yo-yo is a fleeting craze
That vanishes for several years,
Like a forgotten song or phrase,
Then just as weirdly reappears.

So next time they are lost from view
I'll curb the urge to sigh, Alack!
Remembering that's what yo-yos do —
They go away and then come back.

CHRISTMAS

Christmas isn't love and snow;
It's several Sundays in a row,
And family spats across mince pies
As mental care admissions rise.

STICK UP YOUR STOCKINGS!
THIS SANTA IS LOADED!

Christmas comes but once a year —
I can't recall who said it.
I only know that, when it's here,
Invariably I dread it.
      Peace and goodwill are all very well;
      I wish the whole world could be friends.
      But this is the season of buy and sell
      And there my philanthropy ends.
            As the snow in the high street turns to slush
            So my heart turns to ice in the Christmas crush.

For cousins and lovers and mothers and brothers
Are hotly pursuing on lunatic wings
The unpleasant pleasure of buying for others
Dozens of disparate, desperate 'things'.
      Something for Marilyn, Daryl 'n Carolyn.
      What in the shelves of the shops would they like?
      An overnight hold-all to stash their apparel in?
      A pop-up toaster? A fold-away bike?
            A carpenter's box that's also a stool?
            A digital watch that's also a pen?
            A camera to capture this merry Yule?
            Or a manly shoulder-bag – for men?

There are kits for the cunning, sweets for the sweet,
CDs for rock or baroque music-lovers,
Things without which no homes are complete,
Like miniature Bibles and telephone covers.
    There's a biscuit tin or a marble egg
    To share an unforgettable day with,
    Toys that cost parents an arm and a leg
    Which kids quite flatly refuse to play with.
        Things to swallow, to sprinkle, to spray,
        To work, to drive, loll, jog or sleep in,
        Things you immediately throw away,
        And things to keep – all the things you keep – in.

Don't stop to wonder where it'll end.
Spend, spend in mounting amounts,
To prove to all who call you friend
It isn't the thought, it's the gift that counts.
    Slippers and cardies and cuff-links and socks,
    Paperweights, paperbacks, dominoes, dice.
    Anything you can get into a box.
    Snap them up, wrap them up. Rub off the price.
        "What's this? It isn't. It is. It's – yes!
        Well I never! What a surprise!
        It's just what I wanted. How did you guess?"
        Wrong colour, wrong fabric, wrong brand,
            wrong size.

Yes, Christmas comes but once a year
But never when prices are falling.
Oh call me cynical, sour, near.
I call it appalling.
    The *business* of Christmas is simply ridiculous
    And I lampoon the cries of little Saint Niculous.

Now, Harrods! Now, Tescoes! Now, Barkers! Now, Boots!
Off, Bathsalts! Off, Babycham! Shampoo! Cheroots!
From poshest emporium to lowest street stall,
Now, go away, go away, go away all
     You frantic shoppers, you frenzied spenders,
     Armed to your back-teeth with pounds and pence!
     Hence with your grinders and mixers and blenders,
     Your tinsel and turkeys and tarts. I say hence!

Go away digital calculators,
Clocks whose numbers greenly glow,
Space games, radios, torches, vibrators,
Plus the batteries to make all the flaming things go!
     Go away books by Hollywood stars,
     Swanson and Mason and Bergman and Niven.
     Go away chocolates, nuts and cigars.
     Come back Scrooge. All is forgiven.

Christmas 1980

THE BIG BUILD-UP

The dentist said my gums were under attack.
"Look in the mirror," she said, and tapped the plaque.
I looked. There was the plaque. I'd no idea.
It said, "The writer H G Wells lived here".

ORAL IMPERATIVE

"THIS MOUTH-WASH FIGHTS PLAQUE.
USE AFTER EVERY MEAL.
IT LEAVES YOUR MOUTH FEELING FRESH."

I wonder how my mouth will feel.

GO FORTH AND MULTI-BUY

Mildred shops when life begins to pall.
She grabs her bag and turns her face to the mall.

NOT WAVING BUT YAWNING

Life's too short for bores? Wrong.
Quite the reverse. Life's too long.

MEA CULPA

Though reasonably robust,
I've lost the will to dust.

HOW IS YOUR SEAT?

Crammed in crowded long haul planes,
We dine and deeply clog our veins.
Seated thus we also find
That travel broadens the behind.

HOLD IT RIGHT THERE

They gazed at one another
Across the double bed,
And a total lack of interest
Reared its ugly head.

MERCIFUL HEAVENS

Believe in God; his every word
Is strictly bona fide.
He weeps for the fall of the smallest bird
And eats fish on Friday.

AN ACTOR DESPAIRS

He made an appointment with success;
She blew him a promising kiss.
But the only appointment he managed to get
Was the kind that begins with dis.

DON'T JUST SIT THERE

"Pollution's crap. The air stinks.
It wrecks the quality of our lives.
It's got to stop," he often thinks
In traffic jams, as he drives.

ME TARZAN, YOU LOLLIPOP LADY

That car's safari bull-bar frame
In accidents will kill or maim,
Essential in the urban wild
To save you from a charging child.

WHAT DID YOU BREATHE AT SCHOOL TODAY?

Boys and girls come out to play,
The air is full of lead today.
On second thoughts, you'd better stay
At home with an inhaler spray.

BABY TALK

In heaven two guardian angels met and smiled;
The soul in each one's care had birthed a child.
"I'm so delighted," said the first protector.
"Seven pounds. A Public Health Inspector."
"Mine had a girl, but here's the big surprise.
A black poet who'll win a Nobel Prize."

Beside their cloud hovered a silent third,
Who tried to force a smile at what she heard.
"Mine was alone last night, and lost her life
Cutting herself open with a knife.
She held on bravely, till the child arrived—
A serial killer. Weak, but he survived."

GREEK RUINS

King Oedipus suffered from self-deceit.
His name means 'Him with the swollen feet.'
He murdered his father and married his mother.
His son, Polynices, was also his brother.

The playwright, Aeschylus, dropped down dead
When a turtle was dropped on his hairless head
By an eagle who thought his head was a rock.
The turtle, Doris, died of shock.

Polyphemus the Cyclops, books disclose,
Had one red eye above his nose.
It was round and moist and hyper-active.
His wink, they say, was not attractive.

Penelope kept her beaux at bay
By weaving a tapestry all the long day.
"I'll wed," she said, "when I've snipped the last thread."
Then she'd pick it to pieces and pop off to bed.

Her husband, Odysseus, was always abroad,
Poking in caves for the Tourist Board,
Cruising the coast's bewitching environs,
And waxing wild at the song of the sirens.

The pipes of Pan ravished Arcadia
When woods were wilder and streams cascadier.
His morals were far from Puritanic
And frequently caused a picturesque panic.

The Furies were antisocial creatures
With scarcely any redeeming features.
They'd hound and howl and spit and fret
And flatly refuse to forgive and forget.

Quite a different kettle of fish
Was Helen of Sparta. She was a dish.
She ran away with a Trojan boy.
Good news for Paris. Bad news for Troy.

The Goddess of Love, Aphrodite,
Visited shepherds in naught but a nightie
And almost invented the social whirl.
A very, *very* popular girl.

An amazing career had the Princess Medea
Who amassed an enchanting pharmacopoeia.
With cauldron aboil and a midnight song
She did people in with alarming élan.

The Minotaur lived in a maze in Crete
With bovine bust and human feet.
He'd prowl its passages, hoping to meet you,
Bellow "Hello!" then proceed to eat you.

Orpheus played the lyre or harp.
He was never flat and never sharp.
His music provided aid and succour
To all the world – a peerless plucker.

Medusa had snakes instead of hair
And lord knows what for a derrière.
A striking girl. You couldn't miss her.
You turned to stone if you saw her kisser.

"I was given," said Midas, "the golden touch,
But didn't enjoy it much, as such.
You can't teach tricks to a solid gold parrot,
Or munch an eighteen carat carrot."

Zeus set an immoral tone
For those assembled round his throne.
His favourite sport has several names
But isn't in the Olympic games.

SONNET 2001

How do I love thee? Let me count the ways
Thou makest not my crabbed flesh to creep.
Thou dost not batter me with wicker trays.
Thou dost not yodel "My Way" in thy sleep.

    I thee thus love because thou'rt not a monk;
    Upon thy knees thou dost not pray for weeks.
    Thou dost not spike thy hair up as yon punk,
    Nor, hamster-like, store food inside thy cheeks.

For thee my pregnant love thus bravely swaggers;
Thou art not like a wart-hog, fierce and fat.
Thou dost not pick thy teeth with iron daggers,
Nor eatest daily papers like a rat.

    Thus I loveth, swearing I never won'teth,
    All thou weren'teth, aren'teth, can'teth and don'teth.

P. Eth. I muth get to the dentith.

59

PLAY NICELY

"My brother plays the piano like Franz Liszt,
But I'm a shocking pianist," she hissed.
"I'm going crazy, doctor. What do you think?"
"A case of pianist envy," said her shrink.

SHOWING YOUR TRUE COLOURS

"Woe is me! Alack the day!
My pubic hairs are going grey!"
So I cried at forty-odd,
Followed by groans of "Oh dear God."
A shocking, mocking mid-life pang —
Salt had joined the pepper gang.
As above, so below
Fell those follicking flakes of snow.
"Oh curly plight! Oh all is lost!
Oh curse this early, pearly frost!"
I tugged those twirly traitors out,
Thinking to foil Dame Nature's rout,
Until one day – alas the sight –
Less brown hove into view than white.
Well, now near sixty, boys and girls,
There's nought but argentiferous curls.
But who gives tuppence? Fiddle-dee-dee.
They're there. They're fine. They're mine. They're me.

Those of a delicate, nervous brain
Should read no more, or not complain.
I've lady friends dyed to the roots
With hues from bottles bought at Boots.
As they're bending o'er their sinks,
Bottle in hand, do they, one thinks,
Apply the eye-deceiving mixture
To that lower hirsute fixture?

One wonders, do they . . ? *Do* they? Yes?
I guess I'll simply have to guess.
How can one phrase a question like that
Without offence? "How grey's your twat?"

GENTS

From Cain
To John Wayne,
It's been true.
In the loo
Guys
Of whatever size
Sprinkle
When they tinkle.

Polished tile?
Tufted pile?
Forget it.
They wet it.
Chaps always have,
In bog or lav,
Be it Jean-Paul Sartre
Or Frank Sinatra.

Carefree aim
Is partly to blame
As Nick
And Dick
Ignore
The floor.
Craig and Chris'll
Lean back and whistle,
Their minds and brains
On higher planes.

Ned,
Fred
Or Ted
  Shows,
  Flows
  And goes.

Harry,
Larry
Or Gary
  Flashes,
  Splashes
  And dashes.

Barely any
Lenny
Or Kenny
  Stops
  And mops
  His drops.
    He drips
    From the hips
    And zips.

That's final.
Round bowl or urinal,
Your average Lionel
Stereotype
Neglects to wipe.

Maybe one in ten
Bill or Ben
Checks
For specks
And erases
His traces.
  The rest,
  At best,
  Rarely ever
  Endeavour.

They pee
And flee.
With a tweak and shake
Of their trouser snake
They split.
To wit –
That's it.

Most Macks
And Jacks
And Rons
And Dons
Who choose
To use
The toilet.
Spoil it.

THE SHOCK OF THE OLD

Clever, elastic, sensitive skin
Seals you and keeps you all the way in.
Whether your build is stick-like or stout,
Skin stops you falling all the way out.
It hinges and corners at elbow and hip,
As snug as a bug and as smart as a whip.
It wraps and contains you in unbroken pieces,
But sadly, with age, it textures and creases.
It hangs down in pleats like Victorian swags
As your eyes grow bags and your big end sags.
It dangles in fronds, in webbing and flaps
More contoured than Ordnance Survey Maps,
Until it resembles rumpled bedding
The morning after a riotous wedding.

A freckle is charming; what's not is a blotch,
As you will discover if you wait and watch.
Your hands, your brow, your cheek and your pate
Will mottle like foxing if you watch and wait.
Hence the pejorative phrase 'the old trout',
Which doesn't mean one who swims deftly about.
Yes, freckles are pretty, if kept in their place,
But not if they're huge and obscure half your face,
Like splashes of mud the colour of liver,
Causing the owner to blanch and to quiver.
Blanch though ye might, and as pale as a ghost,
It won't send them packing for you are their host.
They march in like guests who arrive uninvited,
Thronging your surfaces, bold and excited.

Veins pop up, varicose, purple and broken.
Yes, it's the real thing, not just the token.
Vain are your protests, cosmetic your ploys,
Plastic your surgeon, diminished your joys.
So what with the wrinkles, the sags and the blotches,
Skin's quite an eyeful if one waits and watches.

Life's packed with challenges. Growing old's one,
But doing it flawlessly cannot be done.
Gracefully, yes, your honour redeeming,
And much less exhausting than kicking and screaming.
Humanity's grass and wither we will,
But do it with energy, spirit and skill.
The light may be dying through illness or age,
But don't rail against it with impotent rage.
Shaking your fist cuts no helpful ice;
Heed not the crapulent poet's advice.
Conversely don't crumple and whimper and dither.
Wither with vigour, vivaciously wither,
Approaching your coming of eld with boldness,
Facing full frontal the prospect of oldness.
Your skin is the key. It shows what's within –
The beauty of soul that lies under the skin.
So wrinkle with dignity, humour and pride,
Preserving the unblemished features inside.
The light of your wisdom, humanity, grace
Will shine from your skin like the sun on your face.

This isn't my theory; it's what I've been told,
So hell only knows what I'll say when I'm old.

FETCHING PANTS

Beshrew my heart, I never fail
To prove a sucker for a sale.
But when I see a catalogue
I should be chained up like a dog.

Bargain chinos beckoned. Beige.
Somewhere between taupe and greige.
"Useful trousers those," thought I.
"Why not go ahead and buy.

"They are casual and smart.
They'll be precious to my heart;
Good to sit or run around in,
Work or play or just be found in.

"Yes," I thought, "They'll suit me fine.
I won't rest till they are mine.
I'll not cease from mental strife
Till they're the fabric of my life.

"By train, by plane, by land or sea,
Bring those very pants to me!
I simply will not be denied them.
Me, me, me must be inside them!"

I ordered them. O.K. so far.
As Shakespeare said, "Well there you are."
Three weeks later they arrived.
I'd been through hell but I'd survived.

I slipped them on. That pair of slacks
Hung from my hips like empty sacks.
A tiny frown replaced my smile.
Where was the cut? Where was the style?

I stood like this, I stood like that
To like what I was looking at.
I didn't. I did not admire
My recently acquired attire.

They weren't fetching, sharp nor chic,
Nor no boon to my physique.
As I moved about they creased
And that creasing never ceased.

When I sat my knee-cap joints
Poked out like spiky compass points.
I looked hard and I looked long.
Had they got the order wrong?

The mystery would not unravel.
Was it, like wine, some slacks don't travel?
The photo showed the same I had
But not the same was what they clad.

"Dear oh dear," I sighed, "Oh dear.
They don't suit me, that's quite clear."
Then I paused for I had found
It was the other way around.

"It is *I* who don't suit *them*!
That is where my problems stem.
It is *me* they don't look good on.
Look at what those pants were stood on.

"He's a burly, manly man,
Burnished with a perfect tan.
Pants he puts on don't look baggy.
They looked fitted, tough and craggy.

"He is shirtless, he is active,
Sturdy, strapping and attractive.
I am not and that's the trouble.
I have no designer stubble.

"With two ladies he cavorts.
They're in snazzy running shorts.
The thoughts he thinks are happy thoughts
As he cavorts with girls in shorts.

"He smiles through centre-parted hair,
Finely and divinely fair.
Has he problems? He has not.
Has he confidence? A lot.

"A god-like champion of sports
Of both the out and indoor sorts,
Running blithely on a beach
On a planet out of reach.

"He's a better shape than me.
He has a shape that you can see.
In fact, the fact you can't escape
Is *he* has what you'd call a shape.

"He has arms that are not thin,
Lustrous hair where I have skin,
A braver brow, a squarer chin,
A neater nose, a firmer grin,

"Whiter teeth and clearer eyes,
Broader shoulders, thicker thighs.
It's a build you'd kill to stand in,
And a face you don't kick sand in.

"He has the tightest, rippliest tummy,
And I'm sure, the proudest mummy.
I take less sartorial room
Than a stood up kitchen broom.

"And of course, what's even loonier,
He is thirty years my junior.
That is why those pants look good.
It's on what those pants are stood.

"God-like, muscularly trim,
Not a stranger to the gym,
He would grace a plastic sack!"
So I sent the buggers back.

>Clothes can cleverly disguise
>Limbs of an imperfect size.
>But at best you only hide them.
>Clothes don't change what's placed inside them.

TOP DRAWERS, BOTTOM DRAWERS

At an auction sale in Camden Town
I waved to someone and – blow me down
Acquired a pair of Victorian bloomers,
Surrounding which were ribbons and rumours
Concerning their original sporter –
No less than Edward Hanover's daughter.
Plain in style, impeccably sewn,
Smelling faintly of eau-de-Cologne,
They were short in the leg but fairly wide,
With the Balmoral coat of arms at one side.
She wore them, according to one suggestion,
One morning when Albert popped the question,
Holding thereafter a special place
In her heart of hearts and her lawn and lace,
For whenever they touched her tender behind
Albert's wooing sprang to mind!
— Which can't be true. However prim,
She was the one who proposed to *him*
Because of her superior status
In the social apparatus.
However, she donned them with private delight
As the occasion or time felt right –
Christenings of her daughters and sons,
Funerals of her beloved ones,
Weddings and birthday celebrations,
Openings of bridges and railway stations,
Trooping the Colour on Horse Guards Parade,
Musical evenings when Mendelssohn played,

And some aver, though reports are confused,
She wore them when she was not amused.
But whenever they clad her, if clad her they did,
I bagged them in my inadvertent bid,
And by George, it gives me, I have to confess,
A fundamental kick to possess
The nearest object one can own
To that which sat on Victoria's throne.

BREAK A LEG

Ballet dancers are brave and tough
And that's no wicked perjury.
If I attempted leaps like that,
I'd need immediate surgery.

HIDDEN ASSETS

Pearl acquired arthritic hip-joints
Stripping in unheated clip-joints
And a nasty chesty cough,
As they shouted, 'Get 'em off!'

Wisely, she retired to Bude
On the savings she accrued,
Modestly and warmly swathed,
Stripping only when she bathed.

THINK ABOUT IT

Between the clever and the wise
If you look close you'll see a distance
Of considerable size,
Despite their obvious coexistence.

The world is full of clever sticks
Who like to show off and surprise
An audience with amazing tricks
But who are very far from wise.

Of all the examples one may note
Showing the gap between the two,
The wise and clever, may I quote
Just the following one to you?

It's clever, you'll agree I know,
Demanding stamina and grace,
To spin repeatedly on one toe
And not to topple flat on your face,

Executing perfect sets
In time to music on a stage
Of dizzying, dazzling pirouettes —
A tour de force at any age.

Oh yes. To spin like that is *clever*,
Clever as the great Fonteyn,
But hardly a *wise* thing, however,
To do in the path of an on-coming train.

WHAT IS THE MATTER?!

An atom, though extremely small,
Contains mainly nothing at all.
What could possibly be eerier
Than its hollow, weird interior?
Inside, its nucleus sits at home
The size of a pea in St. Peter's dome.
It hangs there like the holy grail,
Taking no calls, getting no mail,
Around it drafty, echoing space;
No rugs, no lamps, no fireplace,
No bowls of fruit, no dining chairs,
No fitted shelves, no loo, no stairs,
No bed for putting slippers under,
No room for guests. No guests. No wonder

I can picture places cheerier
Such as scrubland in Siberia;
But dear oh dear, what I'm afraid of
Are the things the atom's *made* of,
Elements beyond my thinking,
Stuff that leaves me gasping, blinking.

When you are *sub*-atomy
You have no anatomy.
Very little you possess;
Barely a forwarding address.

They seek 'em here, they seek 'em there,
They seek those photons everywhere.
Are they particles or waves?
Those demned elusive, slippery knaves!

I don't like mechanics quantum.
You can keep 'em. Me no want 'em.
Wouldn't touch'em. Never use'em.
If they're offered, I refuse 'em.

Maybe I'm a fool to hate
What I can't appreciate,
But I don't like their crazy games.
I don't even like their names —
Lepton, hadron, meson, boson;
Not on me your boson grows on.
Call me an ungracious grouse
But I won't have one in the house.
In the street, I look right though them.
I avoid them, I eschew them.
If we met down some dark alley,
You can bet I wouldn't dally.
Fancy coming face to face
When someones face is empty space!

Those peculiar, fiddly particles
Are no ordinary articles;
They're confusing and confounding,
Creepy, spooky and astounding,
Way beyond my comprehension,
Items from the fifth dimension!
No, not items, but *events*,
And events that make no sense!
Far too small to call them specks,
They've no colour, shape or sex.

Are they tangible? Not them.
Can you view them like a gem
Held between the thumb and finger?
Not those babies; they don't linger.
All you get is just a trace
Of dots they leave . . . where they took place!
Like a disembodied band
Of visitors from Wonderland;
Not an Is, more of a Was
Whizzing from the Land of Oz.

I can just imagine that
As something like my neighbour's cat
Which does exist because I find
Evidence it leaves behind,
Proving, though it's never seen,
That's *exactly* where it's . . . been.

Unlike balls, you can't control them,
Dribble, juggle, bounce or bowl them.
Un-pick-upable, un-put-backable,
Their bizarreness is implacable.
And, because they're undetectable,
Ergo, they are uncollectable,
Unlike stamps or pretty shells,
Jet-planes, Renoirs or hotels.

You can't mount or sell or swap them,
Polish, dangle, drill or drop them,
Bind them, frame them or display them,
Carve them, paint them or inlay them,
Heap them up in little piles
Store them in your office files.
You can't slip one in your pocket,
Keep one in a silver locket,

Pin one in your coat lapel,
Toss one down a wishing-well.
They're no good as gifts for nieces,
Or to stick on mantlepieces.
Due to their unstable traits,
They make lousy paper weights.

They're no sooner come than gone.
Oh scientist – *What's going on*?

Pray don't say I've overdone things
When I shun these things as UN-things.
Imprecise, uncertain, random,
I can't stand or understand 'em.
So I beg you, physicist,
Lift this mystifying mist.
If you'd be so awfully kind,
Un-boggle, please, my boggled mind.
Teach me not to be alarmed;
Tell me why you call some charmed.
Are they pleasant and amusing
Or more staggeringly confusing?
Speak in language clear to me.
Render quanta dear to me.
If you don't, I can't begin
To get inside their tiny skin.
Even hugely magnified,
They have no skin to *get* inside!

Small is beautiful is a platitude
Which does not sum up my attitude.
My response is very wary.
Sub-atomic life is scary.

WHO PUT THE FUN IN PROFUNDITY?

They say truth lies beneath the visible —
That truth is at the bottom of it all.
I say their talk of truth is risible,
And what is all? A box, a bag, a wall?

All has no bottom nor indeed no top,
No front, no rear, no side, no width, no height.
It's not a shelf or counter in a shop
Where truth is kept discreetly out of sight.

So what I say is, I say it's unwise
To say the truth lies here or anywhere,
Or specify its colour, shape or size.
No no. Let's say, truth lies – and leave it there.

      The rainbow is an optical illusion
      Existing only relative to you;
      A perfect metaphor for our confusion —
      It is and isn't there. And that is true.

KEEP GOING TILL YOU HEAR 'CUT'.

Life is one long master-shot,
No retakes or reverses.
You have to improvise like hell
'Cause nobody rehearses.

> Badly staged and oddly cast,
> Your big scenes aren't directed.
> You have to do them off the cuff,
> Sometimes when least expected.

There's no well-crafted dialogue,
And stories aren't confined
To delicate developments
Some writer had in mind.

> You're always tripping over ends
> That aren't tied up or neat.
> Beginnings start where middles are
> And plots are incomplete.

Irony hangs around all day,
Brilliant but ignored.
Good is bad and bad is good;
There's just no just reward.

> You're not told where to move or stand,
> The lighting often stinks,
> Make-up you supply yourself,
> The same for meals and drinks.

Costumes aren't designed for you,
Angles rarely flatter,
Your wisest words aren't audible.
It doesn't seem to matter.

Movie stars can safely suffer.
Life is infinitely tougher
And infinitely much more sweet
Than anything seen from a cinema seat.

CLASSIC

She fell in love with a thunderous thud,
Like a bolt from the blue Olympic peaks,
With a Greek who quickened her English blood,
Boasting the finest of male physiques
But treating her slightly worse than mud.

He favoured a vision way out of her class,
Someone deserving a stunning stud -
The god who graced his looking glass,
Whose golden tan and blonded streaks,
Wash-board tum and buns of steel,
Sculpted lats and cut obliques
Held for him much more appeal.
She sighed, "I've dated other Greeks
But Spiro is my Achilles heel."

THE PHILOSOPHER'S GALLSTONE

We hit the world wailing and weak,
Choking, blind, a hostage to sin,
Struggling to crawl, to walk, to speak,
And then our problems really begin.

        *

Life is a sexually transmitted condition
People are frequently born with, and
Death, while fatal except in remission,
Activates the obituary gland.

        *

Today it appears we are only as old as we look;
So not a slew of consolation there.
As for youth, that carefree, babbling brook,
Alas, mine disappeared into thin hair.

        *

All the best people are strange,
Peculiar, curious or quaint.
In fact, in the turmoil of human exchange,
I've decided there's no one who ain't.

        *

Nice deep breath. The world is up the spout,
Racked by slavery, torture, famine, drought,
War, disease, pollution, racist attacks,
And bring your feet together and relax.

*

While violent crime ought to be peacefully licked,
Vicious habits need to be beaten and kicked.
Beware the silent enemy within;
Sweet inertia is the sapping sin.

*

If only we were all the same,
Models of normal behaviour,
With sexual preferences free of shame
And a filthy great flat in Belgravia.

*

We're up to our eyes in hideous history,
Born, it seems, to fail to learn
Why or how – and here's the mystery —
Tyrants constantly return.

*

For what I hope is ample payment,
Stars today remove their raiment
While the camera pans to places
Where the actors don't have faces.

*

"I hate it when food gets stuck in my teeth."
"In actual fact you should thank your luck
That you've *got* food to *get* stuck in your teeth,
And teeth in which food can *get* stuck."
                                        "Oh shut up."

                        *

For years they've gathered in cupboards to nest,
Their numbers unthinned by depletions.
Now, dithering, cowed, by possessions possessed,
I'm a slave to the ancient Accretions.

                        *

I feel, when I retire to bed
Without a loved one, incomplete.
But there you go, as Shakespeare said.
One thing life is not is neat.

                        *

Getting old can make you fret,
Also what comes after.
So grab each day, and don't forget,
Wrinkles create laughter.

                        *

In subtle ways life can be tough,
Even for those with more than enough
Who luckily sip from a brimming cup,
Yet manage to bugger the whole thing up.

                        *

ODDLY ENOUGH

Cotton is a clever plant;
For just a modest price,
They turn it into shirts and sheets
And duvets. Which is nice.

*

Paper's amazing. We use it for bags,
For letters and leaflets and money and mags
And napkins and books. And as for the press,
What are our newspapers made of? – Yes!

*

Ivy is a clever plant.
It flourishes where others can't.
Concrete sheds are most unsightly;
Ivy hides them. And quite rightly.

*

Pebbles are found on beaches and hills,
As big as potatoes, as little as pills.
What produces a great big boulder?
I'll tell you one day when you're older.

*

Water is a cracking crafty
Creeper into crevices;
It weathers and wears the world into
Grand Canyons and Ben Nevises!

*

Critics are most peculiar creatures,
Blind as moles with pasty features,
Gobbling books and plays and pictures,
Vomiting praise and bile and strictures.

*

We just called them paper-clips.
The French, in their delicious way,
Took then to their hearts and lips
As *les trombones de papier*.

*

Paté de cat is intriguing to eat,
The flavour curiously gamey.
But having gone through all the ones in the street,
I must say it gets a bit samey.

*

Dirt is merely matter out of place,
Such as on one's fingers or one's face.
But in the garden it produces food
And trees and flowers, which improve one's mood.

*

WELL, SHIVER MY TIMBRELS!

Your actual Mozart has no peer
For writing quiet, dainty notes
Specifically for us to hear
The audience cough and clear their throats.

*

Music programmes are a pest;
Readers of them I detest.
They rustle, crackle, fan and flap them
Till I crave to (quietly) slap them.

*

Sergei Rachmaninov, certain critics believe,
Wears his heart too much upon his sleeve
And tears them both too passionately apart.
Maybe. But what a sleeve, and what a heart.

*

Wagner was a clever dick,
Boastful of his performing powers.
"Other composers finish quick,
But I bang on for hours and hours!"

*

I love the music of Poulenc,
Ravel, Fauré and César Franck,
Accompanied, if I am frank,
By a bottle of Gallic plonk.

                *

Sopranos are taller than altos
With longer and narrower throats.
They can't be smaller;
They have to be taller
In order to reach the high notes.

DON'T WATCH THIS SPACE

To galleries tall, to galleries grand
I'm drawn by works of art and craft
And there I often stop and stand
And blankly face *les objets daft*.

HORSES FOR MAIN COURSES

Of *course* one is all for the wild and the free,
But long live the fence and the gate!
The countryside has to be managed, you see,
As most of it's on one's estate.

       *

Shrewd country folk pragmatically determine
Where to stick each beast in each pursuit.
You breed or ride or eat them, or they're vermin,
Yours to torment, poison, hunt or shoot.

       *

Loudly protesting their freedom to ride,
Hunters are hounded with nowhere to hide,
Finally finding, as pressure increases,
Just how it feels to be torn to pieces.

ANTS R US
or
HOW I GOT MY COMEUP-ANTS

Believe it or not, but I was once
A sort of horticultural dunce.
I used to think a garden was for plants.
It only takes a second glance
To see the ones who really wear the pants
Are ants!

Picture this – it's early June;
A gorgeous, golden afternoon.
I stop to take a well-earned break
From toiling with my trowel and rake
And sit me down. The air is warm;
It softens my reclining form,
At rest upon my peaceful lawn,
I yawn.

But not for long. What's that? An itch.
My crawling skin begins to twitch.
The special term for this sensation,
Is formication.
Lifting my shorts, I gasp, I rant —
At an ant!

Another's climbing up my chair;
I spy a third one over there.
The more I look, the more I see
On railing, paling, bush and tree,
In every border, bed and plot,
On every plant, in every pot!

My garden has become infested!
Everywhere I turn, they've nested!
Goodness me, but how their busy
To and froing makes me dizzy.
Then I call myself a fool.
"You fool," I cry, "You've lost your cool.
They're only ants. They do no harm.
Stay calm."

But something weird occurred last week
When my annoyance reached its peak.
I'd bought a weighty urn of stone,
Hoping its gracious, old-world tone
Would dignify and thus enhance
My garden's charm with trailing plants.
And what do I get with quaint romance?
More ants!

Eyeing their tiny muscularity,
All my thoughts were short on charity.
"Ants," I cried, "you aren't romantic.
You're frenetic, frenzied, frantic.
Who could be serene and placid,
Bursting full of formic acid?
Get ye hence and live in France,
Instead of underneath my plants!

"Go! You've got to go," I cried.
But how? I don't use pesticide.

Bribery? No, ants can't be bought.
To prune a leggy story short,
Or snip this little sucker brief,
I tore a page – I can't say leaf –
Out of the Pied Piper's book.
Yes, his ruthless route I took,
And yes, I was as one obsessed,
As now, I'm sure, you must have guessed.

My paranoia knew no bounds
Within those antisocial grounds.
"I'll conjure up harmonic powers,"
I hissed, "to draw them from my flowers
Over the fence and far away
To Basingstoke or Bude or Bray.
I lack his pipe to cast a spell
But I can whistle pretty well.
I'll put those insects in a trance,
Get them to form a line and dance
To Bucks or Berks or Herts or Hants,
Or Canterbury or Penzance,
To Rye or bonny Skye, perchance,
Where several, surely, must have aunts."

That was what my garden needed,
So I whistled as I weeded,
Whistled morning, night and noon
My trance and dance inducing tune,
But whether they were deaf or bored,
All my efforts were ignored,
Until one day, while planting flowers
And whistling solidly for hours,
The strangest, oddest thing occurred.
They paused, and quietly conferred.

All activities were stopped,
Posts abandoned, objects dropped.
They formed a circle close to me
Under the lordly linden tree,
Like a miniature assembly
At a teeny weeny Wembley.

Settled thus and quite sedate,
They held an open air debate,
Speaking in their language, Antic,
Highly formal and pedantic,
Close to Latin, slightly Greekish,
Only more high-pitched and squeakish,
With a nasal, tinny tang,
Or twang.

No one disagreed or yelled
As their crucial talks were held.
Silence fell. One cleared his throat
And put a motion to the vote,
Neatly worded, clearly phrased.
Then, with their antennas raised,
Aye's and no's were duly counted
As the quiet tension mounted.

The vote was carried. Cheers and hoots!
No abstentions, no disputes.
They all looked up. I looked down.
On each ant's face was etched a frown.
The atmosphere became intense,
Excruciating the suspense.

"That's it," I thought, "Here comes the crunch.
The worm has turned. I have a hunch
Those creatures are about to foil
My plan to ban them from my soil."

One beckoned. "Might I have a word?
Stop whistling. You are not a bird.
It's driving everybody barmy.
Furthermore, our little army
Won't be driven from our home
To Reigate, Rotterdam or Rome."

They'd sussed me out! I turned bright red.
And then their little spokesman said,
"Also, for your information,
We are here for the duration,
With no plans to move our nests
Like gypsy folk or weekend guests.
We took a vote. It was, my friend,
Unanimous, and there's an end."
With narrowed eyes, he said,
"We stay. Whistling won't drive us away.
Nothing will. And here's a tip.
Get a grip."

His tone impressed. His words convinced.
I winced.

"Furthermore," he added tartly,
Snapping arms akimbo smartly,
Holding a dramatic pause,
"The problem isn't ours, it's yours!
We've colonised both hemispheres
For several hundred million years,
Through meteor hits, through flood and drought
And we're still here. You work it out.

"There's more of us than you, old sport,
Ten million billion, so it's thought.
Weight for weight, we way outweigh you,
And it looks like we'll outstay you.

"And we're stronger. Think about it.
Could you pull a car? I doubt it.
Another reason our removal
Hasn't met with ant approval
Centres on your evolution
With regard to world pollution.
All you cause is awful trouble
On this interstellar bubble,
Wiping out from here to Kenya
Life that's flourished for millennia!

"We've seen them come, we've seen them go.
You're relatively new, you know.
Your brains are big, but you're short-sighted,
Crude and ethically benighted.
You cut down trees for cattle herds,
Destroying reptiles, rodents, birds,
Spiders, butterflies and bugs,
Plants containing unknown drugs
That you could use to cure you all,
Lost and gone beyond recall."

So far, I thought, it's rather odd
He hasn't mentioned whale or cod.

"Don't get me onto fish!" he thundered.
"Not one ocean's left unplundered!
Mankind's wiped out in a trice
Life on land, sea, air and ice.
History plants the blame on you!
It's a scandal! Shame on you!

"We, in contrast, know our place,
Being a much more balanced race.
We do no damage, cause no strife
Within the complex web of life.

If you question who is greater,
Take it up with your creator.
Think of Eden's tempting fruit;
It wasn't ants who got the boot!

"Ants are quicker, wiser, wittier;
Plus, you must admit we're prettier."
I could have argued with the latter,
But no matter.

"And so, to sum up, my advice is
Leave us ants to our devices."
Thus his tiny tirade ended.
"Nothing personal," he appended,

A hooter sounded. Off they sped
To tub and shrub and garden shed,
In ant affairs preoccupied.
In need of tea, I slunk inside,
Or rather, more correctly, hastened,
Chastened.

An ant had brought me down to size,
Ticked me off and put me wise.
After such an awful earful,
I felt, frankly, almost tearful;
I'll admit it, I was quaking.
Tea pot poised, my hand was shaking.
I'd been duly truly rumbled,
And humbled.

But, as my trembling finger tips
Brought the liquid to my lips,
I woke up with a sudden start,
And a thudding, thumping heart.

I gasped and gulped but oh, good grief,
The relief!

A crazy dream! – induced by heat
While dozing on my garden seat.
A silly dream! – but one I needed.
Nature's warnings must be heeded.
Listen to insects, look at weeds;
Lessons lurk in roots and seeds.
Wise words aren't always loud or tall;
Some pop up very quiet and small,

And sometimes ants in dreams can teach
Those parts that real ants cannot reach.

Now gentle tickles on my ankle
Do not irritate or rankle.
An ant is something on one's foot
Up with which one ought to put.
I hold no grudge, I bear no hate,
For now I gladly tolerate
       Those at whom I used to look askance –
       Ants!

RIDE AT YOUR OWN RISK

Comport yourself
Through life, dear friends
With dignity and grace.
And watch your noses;
As one door closes
Another door will slam in your face.

BEYOND ME

When living ends,
Kind words are said
To sorrowing friends
About the dead,
Sometimes quite unsuitable
Or boring or inscrutable,
Or biblically wise.
Sometimes barefaced lies.

Dear grieving chums,
When my turn comes
Rather than confusing,
Let mine be amusing.

All must cross that great divide,
That valley infinitely wide,
That separating gap
Not found on any map.
I have but one request,
Before my final rest. Or test.

I simply hope, when my turn comes
To take off like an acrobat
Responding to a roll of drums,
Graceful as a swooping bat,
Hurtling from that perilous ridge
Over the gulf that has no bridge,

I hope, when death dispatches me
And dying unattaches me,
And off across that gap I pop
Or swing or sweep
Or swoop or hop,
Or ride or leap
Or jump or drop,
I hope some fucker catches me.

GET AN AFTER LIFE

A chubby man of solid worth,
Let us honour Buddha.
Of all such holy men on earth,
Nobody was goodha.

                    *

Being a being of whom I cannot conceive,
God is one in whom I strain to believe.
I struggle with terms like sin and hell and the host,
But throw in the towel when it comes to the Holy Ghost.

                    *

Flying saucers, like magic spells,
Are hard to find or follow,
But holy water from taps or wells
I really cannot swallow.

                    *

Jesus, one can only suppose,
Like you and me, scratched his nose.
But with all heaven to adore him,
Maybe the angels did it for him.

                    *

With powers holy and divine,
He cured the sick and sinful.
He turned the water into wine
And everyone had a skinful.

*

The Holy Family never quarrel,
Safe in their divine Balmoral.
Blissful, pure, exclusive, grand,
Lo, they sit on each other's right hand.

*

Moses loved his food, did he;
Nothing put him off it.
Thus, in time, he came to be
A self-fulfilling prophet.

*

Reality is here! It moves! It speaks!
But keeps behind a baffling veil, by gum.
A Spanish proverb lifts the hem and peeks.
"Angels don't exist. But there are some."

IS IT POETRY OR VERSE? YES

Dead men don't knit;
They can't get the needles.
But dead men don't quit,
And modern poems don't rhyme.

Dead men don't tan;
Have you seen their skin?
And modern poems don't scan.
A line can have as few or as many words as you like
                  thrown in.

Dead men don't streak;
They're far too sensible.
And modern poems are bleak
And incomprehensible.

Dead men don't snore;
That's one consolation.
And modern poems ignore
capitals syntax punctuation

Of all the poems that ever were,
To some stinkers I've read,
Baffling, cheerless, I'd prefer
The company of the dead.

BLAST!

I'm dead in the grave.
It's nothing o'clock.
I must've dropped off.
Did somebody knock?

What was your question?
How do I feel?
A bit dis-embodied,
Slightly unreal.

Have I regrets?
You want me to list them?
Things that I didn't
And how much I've missed them?

I wish I had learnt
To swim in the sea
With starfish and dolphin
Encouraging me.

I wish I'd enrolled
And sung in a choir
Songs of enchantment,
Despair and desire.

I wish I had danced
The Spanish fandango,
The salsa, the samba,
Lambada and tango.

I wish I'd been wise,
I wish I'd been brave,
And learnt how to love
Like a god and a slave,

Loved and cavorted
While others had slept,
Opened my heart,
Worshipped and wept.

I wish I had done things
For the right reason,
Not been a lackey
To profit and season,

Learnt how to care
For the broken and mad,
And give silent thanks
For the blessings I had.

But more than these things,
Above all, alas,
I wish I'd remembered
To turn off the gas.

PIQUES AND TROUGHS

Grudges are gorgeous to have and to hold,
To help you grow crabby and lonely and old;
So seek out offences and save every slight,
And go to your grave twisted, wretched but right.

NIL DESPERANTO

Upon my gravestone, shadowed from the sun,
Carve, oh carve, for those who've travelled far,
These simple words: Beneath this earth lies one
Who blah blah blah blah blah blah blah blah blah.